FROG moves out of the RAIN FOREST

by Nikki Potts

illustrated by Maarten Lenoir

T0084475

PICTURE WINDOW BOOKS
a capstone imprint

The air is warm.
Food is plentiful.
The neighbors are nice.

It's the rain forest, and it's where Frog calls home.

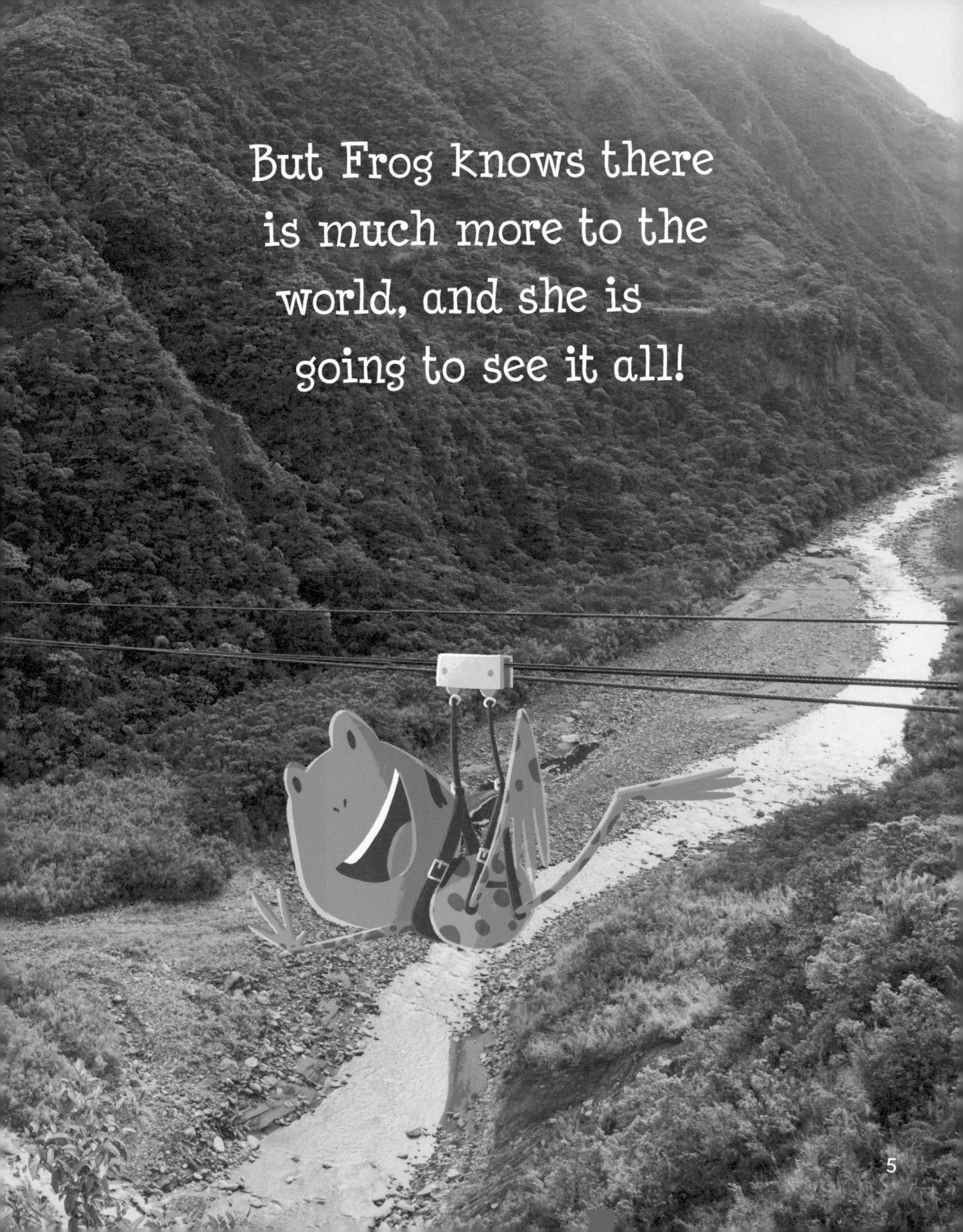

But Frog knows there is much more to the world, and she is going to see it all!

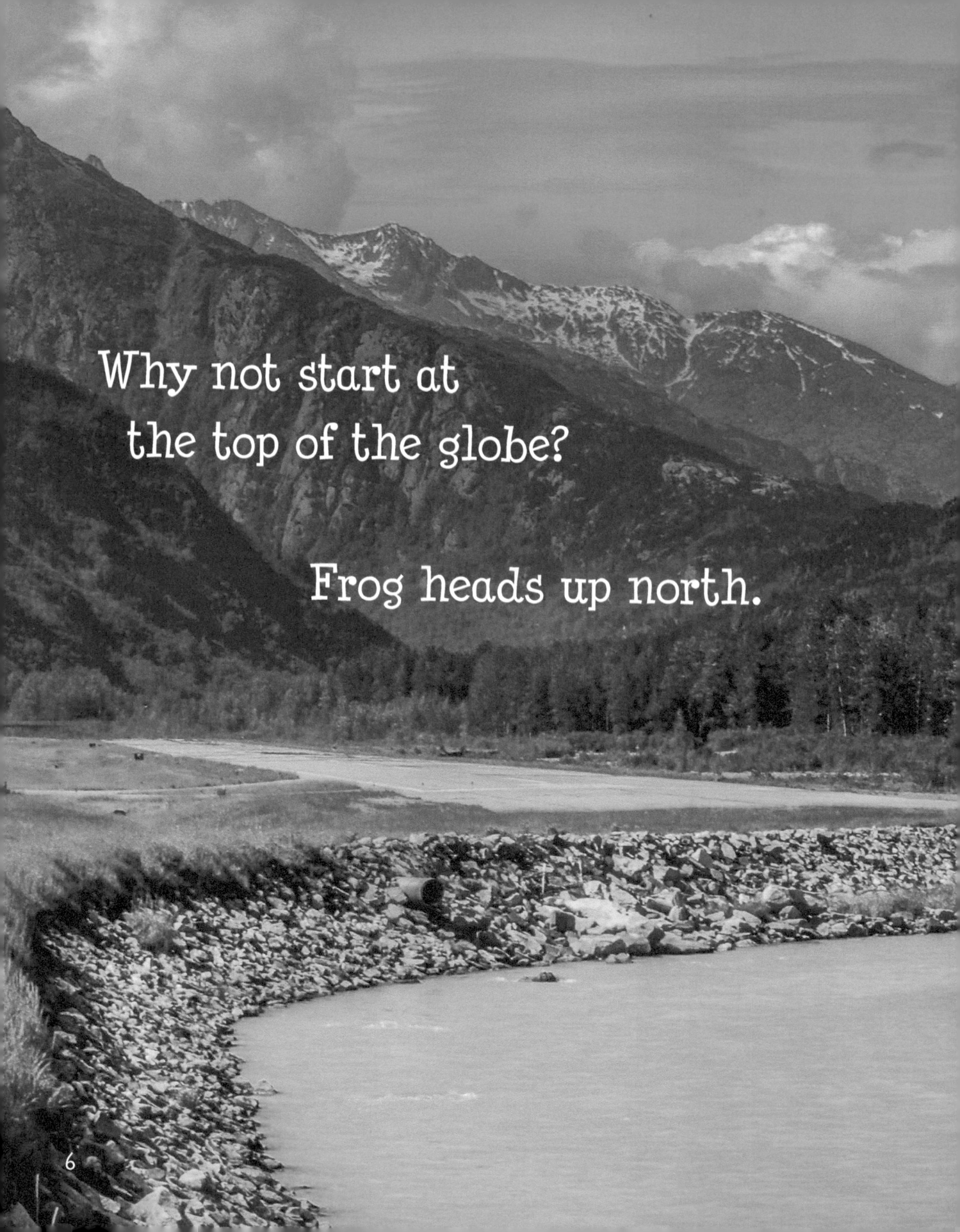

Why not start at
the top of the globe?

Frog heads up north.

The trees remind
her of the rain forest.

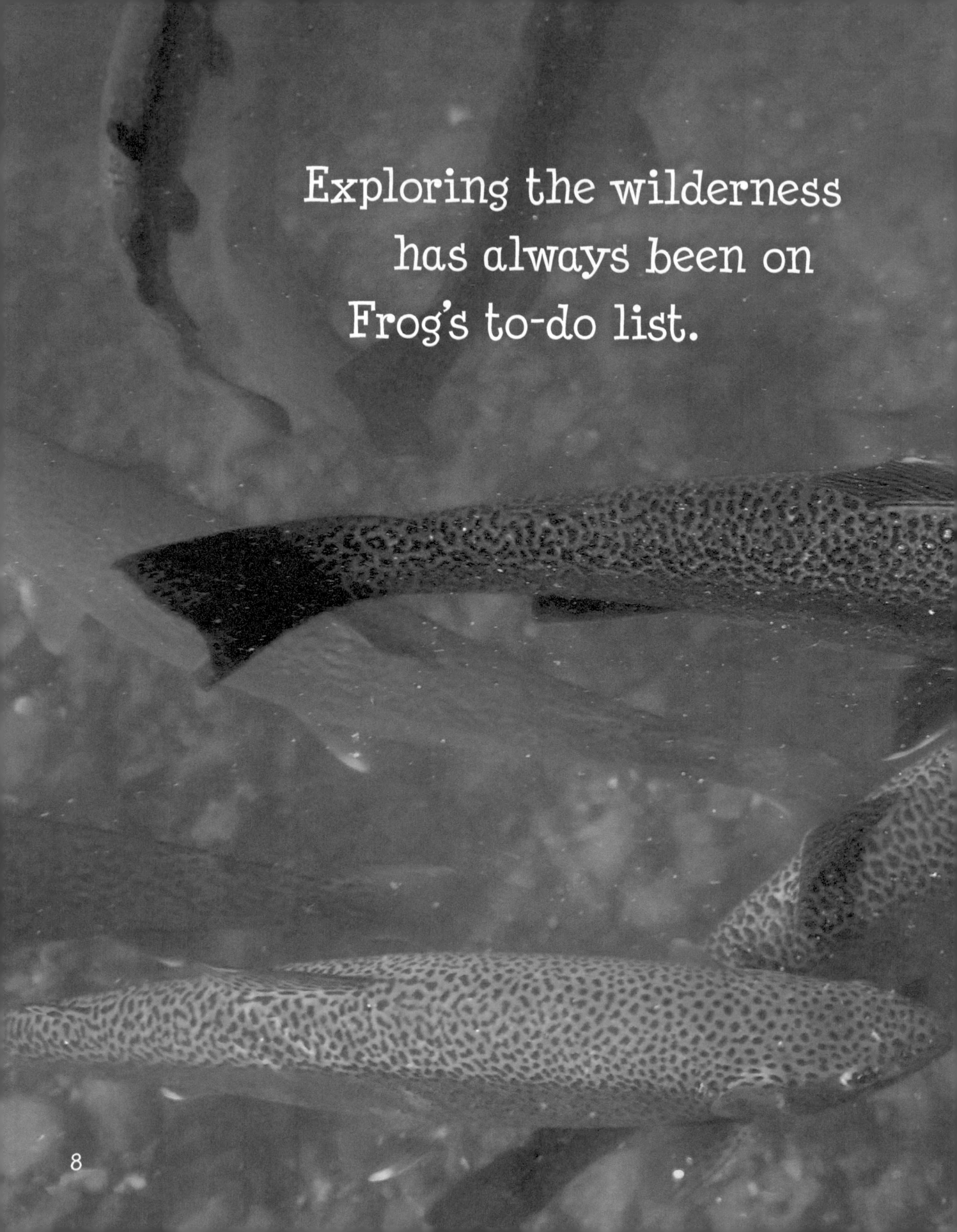

Exploring the wilderness
has always been on
Frog's to-do list.

Who doesn't love
a good adventure?

This is NOT the kind of adventure Frog was imagining.

The great outdoors isn't as great as she thought it was.

Frog needs to
find somewhere
with fewer fish.

The bright lights
and sparkling colors
of the amusement park
are calling!

Nobody rides roller coasters like Frog.
FUN

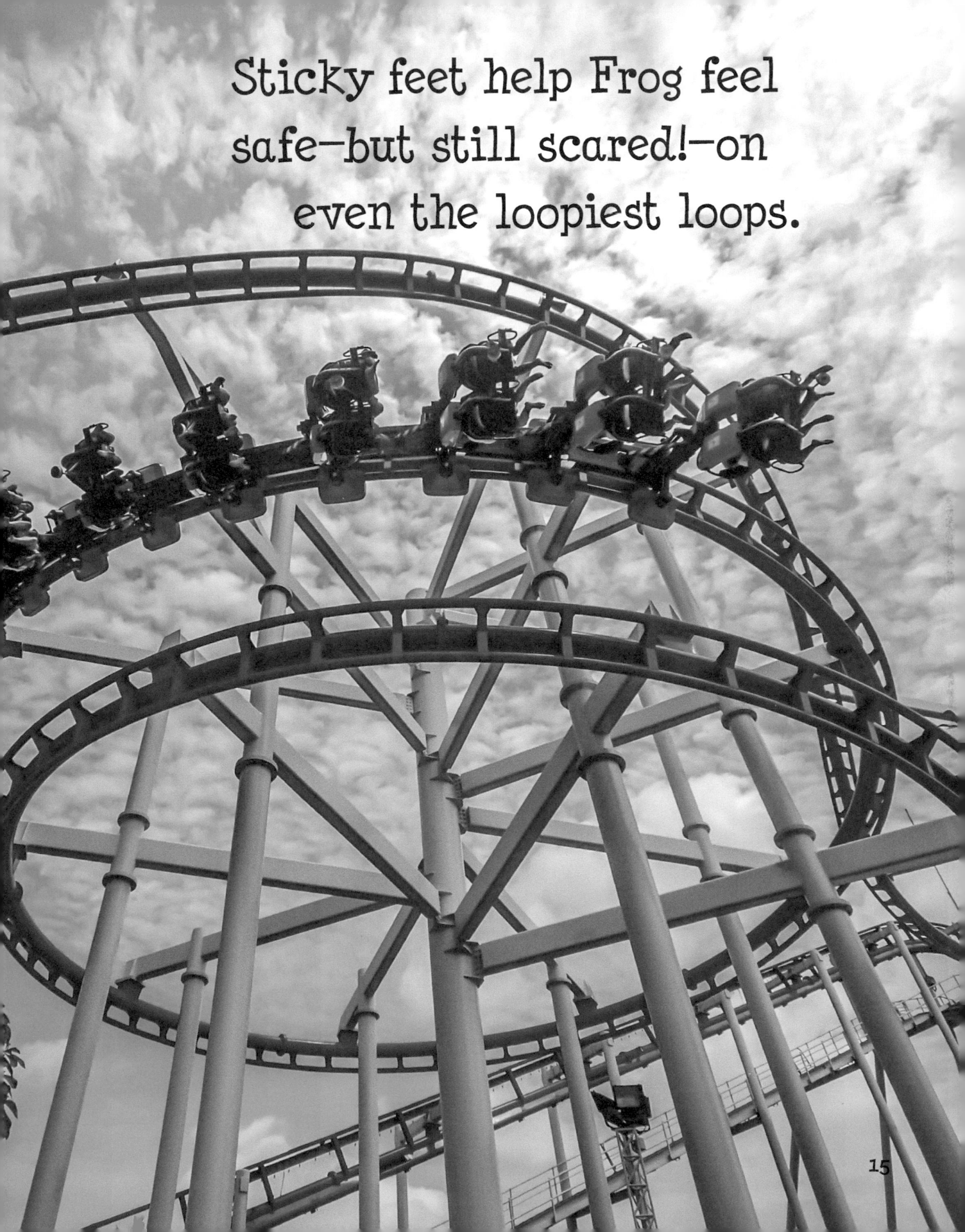

Sticky feet help Frog feel
safe—but still scared!—on
even the loopiest loops.

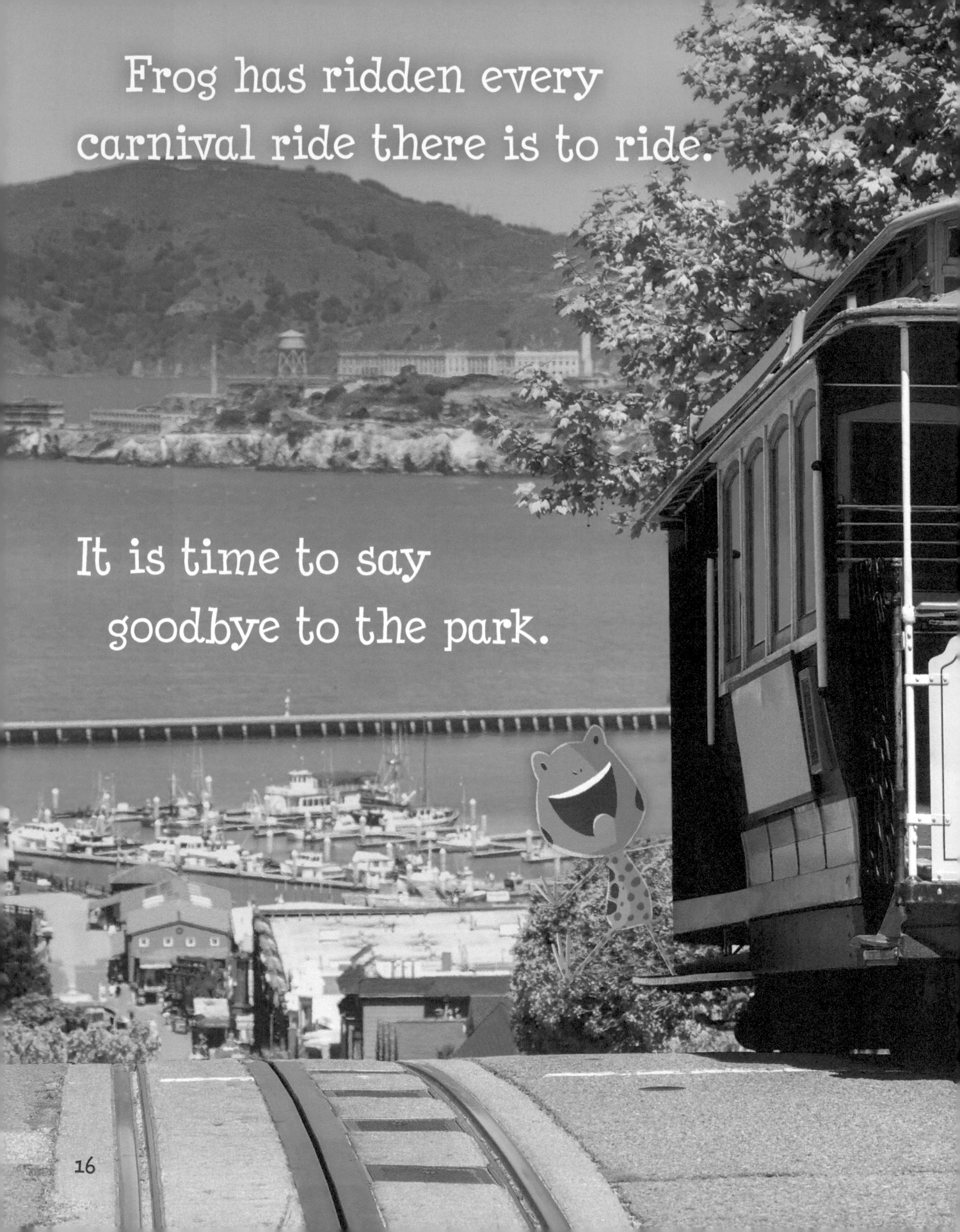

Frog has ridden every carnival ride there is to ride.

It is time to say goodbye to the park.

Off to the next
adventure!

Frog has always wanted
to paint from the top
of a mountain.

And now she has souvenirs to send to froggy friends back home.

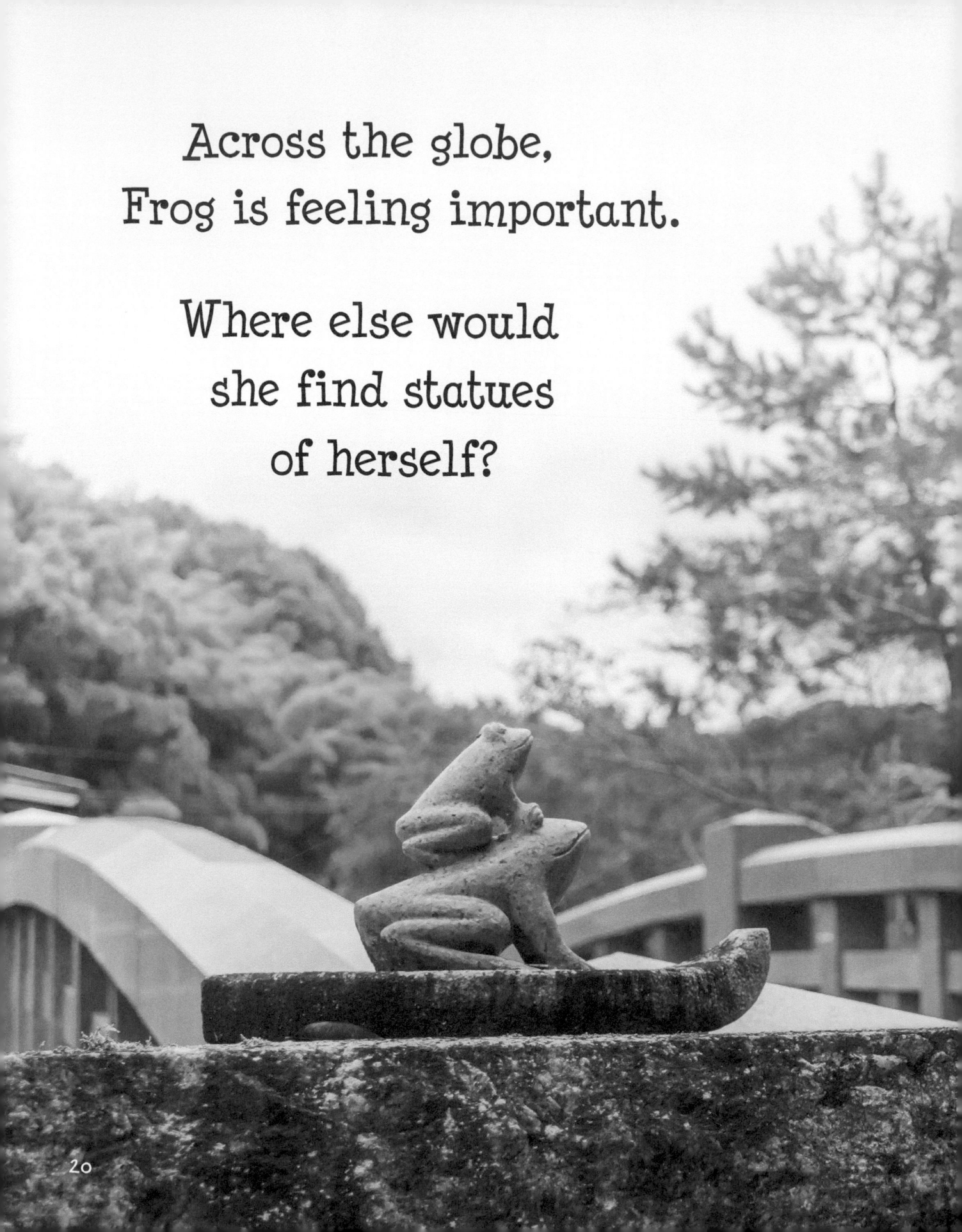

Across the globe,
Frog is feeling important.

Where else would
she find statues
of herself?

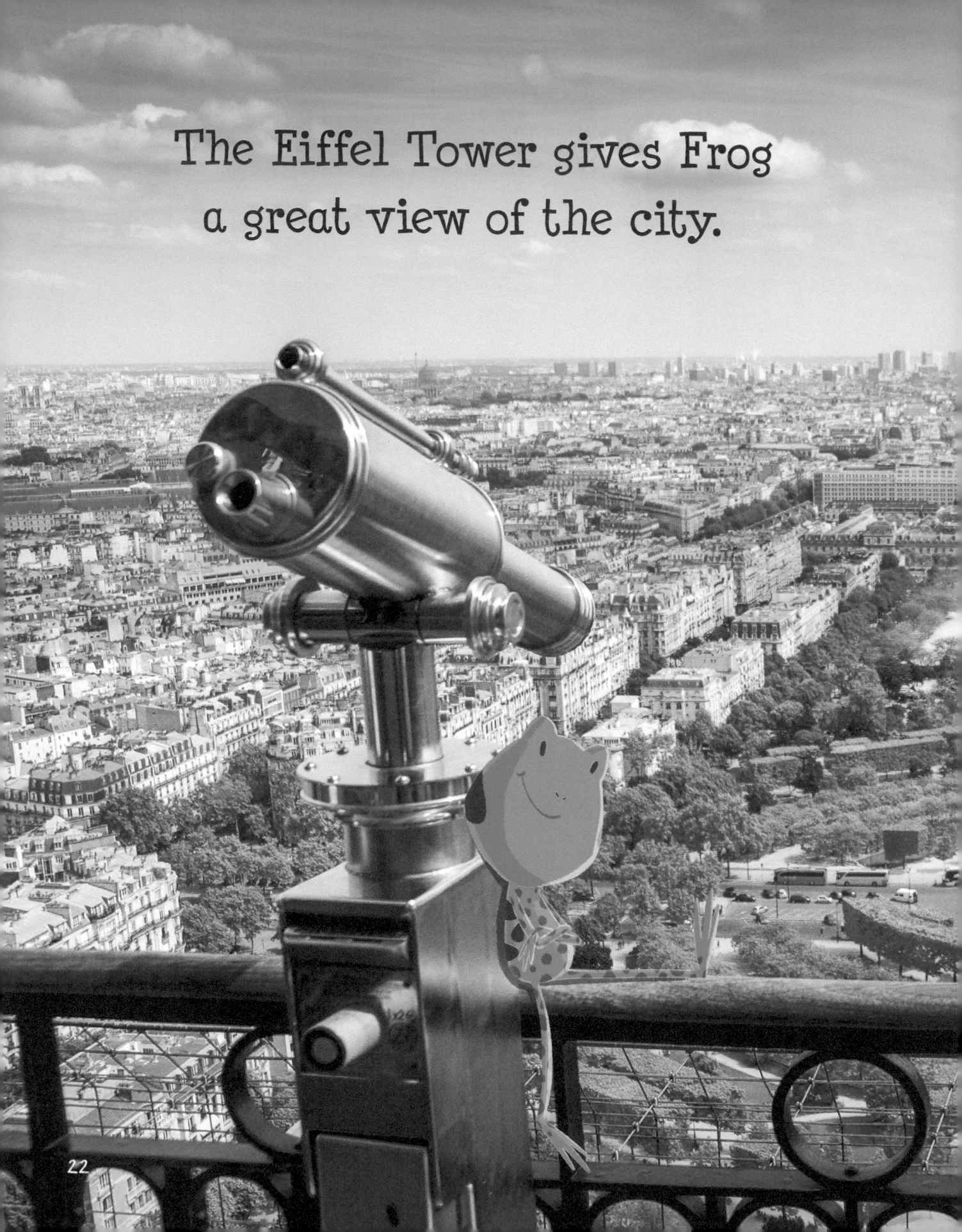

The Eiffel Tower gives Frog
a great view of the city.

Wow!
She has never seen
anything like it.

The giant sequoia trees
are tall too.

Frog feels very small.

So much has been seen and
done during Frog's world tour.

But Frog is homesick.

It's time for vacation to end.

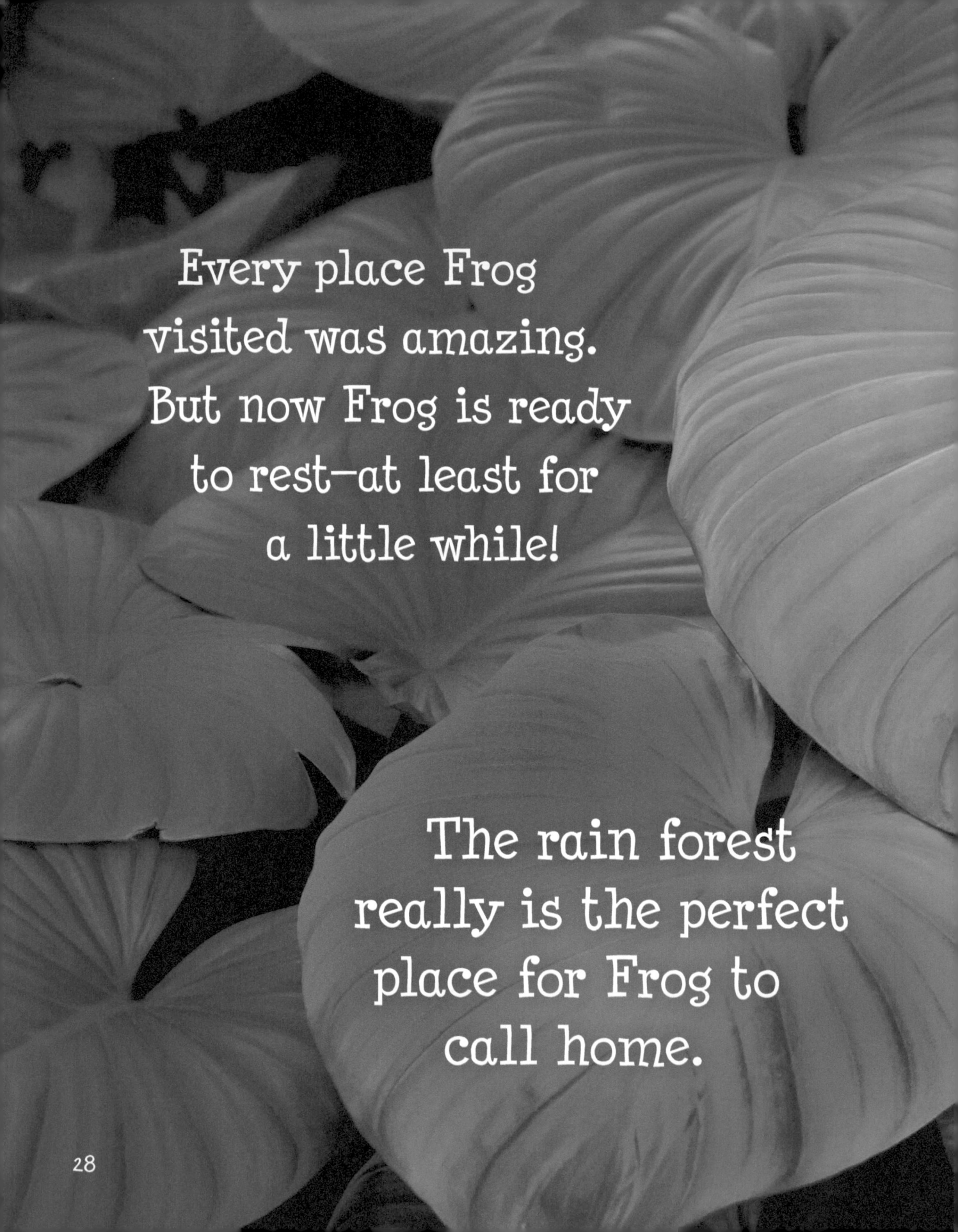

Every place Frog visited was amazing. But now Frog is ready to rest—at least for a little while!

The rain forest really is the perfect place for Frog to call home.

MORE ABOUT POISON DART FROGS

Females leave their tadpoles in spiky tropical plants called bromeliads.

Poison dart frogs are toxic enough to kill. The toxins in their bodies come from the food they eat.

Poison dart frogs do not have webbing between their toes. This means they are not good swimmers.

Poison dart frogs can be one of many bright colors or a combination of colors.

Poison dart frogs catch bugs with their long sticky tongues.

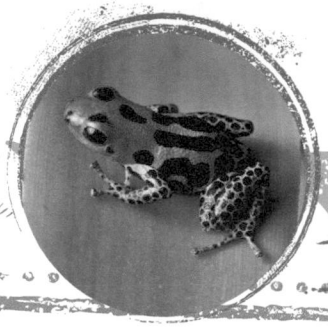

ANIMAL PASSPORT

Name: Poison Dart Frog

Type: amphibian

Habitat: rain forest

Diet: carnivorous; they eat insects and invertebrates

Size: 1 inch (2.54 centimeters)

Weight: 1 ounce (.03 kilograms)

Lifespan: 3 to 15 years

Favorite Activity: climbing

BOOKS IN THIS SERIES

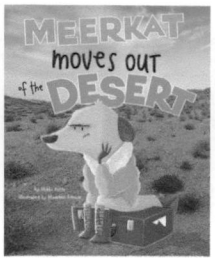

Habitat Hunter is published by Picture Window Books, an imprint of Capstone.
1710 Roe Crest Drive
North Mankato, Minnesota 56003
www.capstonepub.com

Copyright © 2020 by Capstone. All rights reserved. No part of this publication may be reproduced in whole or in part, or stored in a retrieval system, or transmitted in any form or by any means, electronic, mechanical, photocopying, recording, or otherwise, without written permission of the publisher.

Library of Congress Cataloging-in-Publication Data is available on the Library of Congress website.
ISBN: 978-1-9771-1423-5 (library binding)
ISBN: 978-1-9771-2021-2 (paperback)
ISBN: 978-1-9771-1429-7 (eBook PDF)

Summary: Frog is bored with their habitat! Follow Frog as they try out different places to live. Which habitat will make the best home for Frog?

Image Credits
Shutterstock: anek.soowannaphoom, cover, 1, bancika, 22-23, Bonita R. Chester, 8-9, Curioso, 12-13, Dirk Ercken, 31, gowithstock, 14, Logra, 24-25, lunamarina, 16-17, My Life Graphic, 18-19, nelik, 26-27, Nokuro, 2-3, Paul Winterman, 10-11, RoD7, 4-5, Sabaidee, 28-29, SIHASAKPRACHUM, 15, Somporn Wongvichienkul, 20-21, Stephanie Michelle 82, 6-7

Artistic elements: Shutterstock: pingebat, Valeriya_Dor

Editorial Credits
Editor: Mari Bolte; Designer: Kayla Rossow; Media Researcher: Kelly Garvin; Production Specialist: Tori Abraham

All internet sites appearing in back matter were available and accurate when this book was sent to press.

Printed in the United States 5829